scarred HEART

Frea Lee

For the
love
of
my life

you are everything to me -
my heart
and
my soul

table of contents

chapter 1

chapter 2

chapter 3

thank you note
about the book
about the author

chapter 1

you carried me
like a trophy
like precious jewelry
you have always been
there for me
and your love
has to be told

you love me, no need
for reasons
you cared for me
more than your own

repaying you
will take a lifetime
of love, respect and
gratitude

- thank you Mother

when I was young
I told myself not
to fall in love
for I see people
everywhere I look
liquor in hand
crying for another chance
promising to never do the
things that made them cry

still they do it
again and again
never learning

I never wanted to
be famous
I never wanted to
be known nor
heard by many people
all I need is for
you, you alone
to know
I'm here
I exist
and I am
unconditionally
loving you

I couldn't tell you
we were young
and foolish
so I let you go

but time
wasn't too kind
cause you have fallen
in love with another
unkind time

why would you
fix something
that doesn't
need fixing

-why would you fix a love
that's pure
   and true

sitting by the window
in the middle of the night
watching people pass by
with the moon shining up
high

you're with her again
holding hands
listening to a song –
the rhythm of your hearts

if I had told you
I loved you
before she came
into your life
would I be that girl
wrapped in your arms
tonight

stop knocking on
someone else's door
my door has always been
open

I am writing
to you
to tell you how
much I love
and adore you
no, I don't want
you to love me too
but I want you to know
that someone loves you
before she entered your
life and hurt you

-I have always been here for
you

when
is
love
going
to
find
me

I built this fence
for people like you
who can't get enough
drama in your lives
that you have to get
to mine

this white door
between us
is the only thing
that's separating us

-why can't you open your
heart

if I'd be given one chance
one moment
to be with you
I'd simply take your hand
lay on the sands
my head on your chest
listen to your heartbeat
as the soft waves
touch our feet
while the full moon smiles

the truth is
I love you
just like the other
girls around you

your voice
soothes my
very soul
your song
rattles my
very core
your music
tells it all
without a doubt
I am yours

I hope you find me
when you grow
tired of making
people happy

one day
we'll meet on
a busy street
will you even
notice me
a glimpse
a nod
a smile
to spare
or will you
go on
living your
extraordinary life
not wanting
my existence

I will love you
until the next lifetime

I will find you
and I will let you know
I exist

because in this lifetime
it's impossible
to tell you
how much I value you

I will always be here for you
will protect you from
this scary world
we are living in

-to my lovely nephews

I love you
and that's all
you have
to know

I will leave my
heart to you

give it back to me
whole and pure
when we meet again

the sun kisses my skin
soft waves touching my feet
sea breeze whispers
songs of encouragement
I look at you and say
no matter where I go
no matter what I do
in you I'll find my home

a hug so tight
a kiss full of love
a love as vast as the oceans
I'm glad you are the one

I hate thinking of you
it brings me agony

the cracks in my heart
and the cracks
on the floor
are similar

hard to fix
but it still works

a good song
makes you cry
without a reason

it breaks your heart
and it pierces
your soul

as if the song is
written for you
and is meant to
be heard by you

I will love you
today and tomorrow
and if you decide
not to stay
with sorrow I will
step out of
your way

I see people with
their big smiles
and think
why can't those
smiles be mine

just come back
to me safe
and sound
and I'll give you
all the love
you have been
begging her for

the flowers bloom
the birds are singing
still here I am
waiting for the
phone to ring

A love that lasts forever
is all I ever wanted

chapter 2

his eyes sparkle
only for you
don't let them sparkle
for anybody else

I was so busy
looking at you
that I didn't realize
that he was looking
at me the same way
I was looking at you

you asked yourself
why nobody loves you
and why nobody
cares for you

what you don't see
is that he's been loving you
and never stopped caring for
you
but you were too busy
wanting much more than
that

-he wasn't enough for you

a cup of coffee in hand
headsets on my ears
and tears flooding down my
cheeks

memories of you
just keep coming back
haunting me
day and night

rekindling our love
is going to be
a battle of
forgiving
forgetting
and trusting
all over again

a minute ago
we were walking
this long windy road
fingers intertwined
faces full of smiles
and suddenly
you let go
and walked away
without looking back
you left me all alone
and continued walking
on your own

it's been 669 days
          4 hours
          2 minutes
and I haven't moved on
since then.

-it's an illness

if there's a God and
he loves me so much
why'd he let you leave
when He knows
it's you I need

many sunrises and
sunsets have passed
I have grown tired of
waiting for you
to come
and mend this
bleeding heart

repeatedly you'd pick me up
and throw me back
to break to pieces
and repeatedly I'd come back
like a small child
wanting love and affection
from someone who
turned into a monster
or a monster who looked
like a lover

your face
brings me sorrow
your eyes
brings me pain
your lips
brings me bitterness

you
are
my
death

you wanted me to stay
suffer the pain with you
but there's this voice
inside me telling me
to run away - away from
your heart
that is chaotic and unsure

I have hurt you
and I never meant to
he told me that you
and him were over a
long, long time ago
said you kicked him
to the curb along with
his old nasty clothes
didn't see through the lies
because back then
I thought he was mine
I didn't know that
you and him are still
hanging like old times
and now I am kicking
him out
it's either you take
him in or not
I just want to say
forgive me
for not knowing that he's
always been your
man all this time

don't blame yourself
he left because
he wanted to
not because of you
but because of her

if you tell me one more time
that I am useless and dumb
I'd leave this place you call
home
never to look back

-I am so done

I don't need your pity
I have known it for a while
now
that you and her
are sharing the same bond
we used to have
I'll gladly step back
and give her the
place in your arms
I don't need any
explanation of why
of all the girls you could
have fallen in love with
you chose my best friend
I'll leave now
and I'll let you both be
don't come looking for me
it won't help me deal with
the pain you have caused me

the world as pretty as it is
is never fair
never have
never been

if it is indeed fair
like what my mother
and I have been told

then why are you in there
happy
and why am I in here
sad and lonely

a goodbye note
and a kiss on my shoulder
is all you left me

my mind is flooded
by the thoughts of you
wondering if you are
living your life
the way you have always
wanted

-was leaving me worth it

my love for you
is as tall as the mountains
and as deep as the oceans

but you love her
the same way
I love you

if there is
heaven
and hell
on Earth
it's loving you
and not being
loved in return

and it is killing me slowly

what's the purpose
of praying
when all my prayers
are unanswered

what's the use
of loving
when I am always
hurting

if you know me
you know I'll be here
waiting for you
in this cold dark room
where you have left me

take your time
and live your life
I'll just be here
writing our story
with the old typewriter
you have left me

I heard our song
on the radio
on my way home
from work

I can't help but smile
after all this time
you're still the one
my heart is beating for

I am not yours to take
I am his

wasted time
wasted tears

broken wine bottles
broken hearts of gold

when will love stop
hurting us like this

many times I have told you
that she had been unfaithful
but you never listened and
dismissed me
told me I am making up
stories
to destroy the life you are
living

and now I can see
your eyes have been opened
have you seen her with
another
have you seen how her eyes
twinkle for him

she's to be blamed
for the pain
that you are feeling
you were a victim
too blind to see the real her

you've either forgiven her
or decided to forget
how unfaithful she has been

seeing you with her
gives me joy and happiness
to see that you have
found each other again

do you see
my heart

embellished with scars

you told me to wait
and that's what I did
thinking that you'll be there
as you promised

I tried to look for you
even climbed that
big wall of yours

and I saw you standing there
kissing someone else
and it hasn't stopped raining
since

our story
our life
I tried to
write it
then I realized
there was
no you
in my life

I still look up to the stars
not because they're pretty
but they remind me of you
when you lay your head on
my shoulder
on that starry and beautiful
night

a walk on the cliff
made me realize
the world is so big

I am not the only one
hurting

you beat her
as soon as the alcohol
in your glass has drained

the anger seething from
deep inside your soul
tells you it's her fault
that your life turned out
different from your dreams

with every punch and
kick you gave her
with every insult
you threw at her
she accepted it
for she loves you
and is still holding on
to the man she once knew

you knocked on our door
begging us to let you in
black and blue
you were sobbing and shaking
no questions asked
we knew who did this to you
the man whom you love
beat you again
until you're not able to fight
but run away
frightened of what
might happen to you
another knock on the door was heard
it's your man crying and yelling
for you to come back
and forgive him again
we told you not to
but still you let him in
we tried to help you
many times ~ we failed

I can't help but judge and resent you

a smart woman like you
should know better

this cycle of pain, beating,
accepting and forgetting
is going to ruin you

-love is not an excuse to let
others push
         you down so low

you are not a friend
don't act like one
I have been through
a lot because of what you
did and still do
I am better off having an
enemy
than have a friend like you

instead of helping you up
these people you call friends
are going to sink the ship
you are in
for theirs to sail

humans are scary
they say good luck
and congratulations
but what they meant is
"I hope your life is no better
than mine"

your made up stories
about me and my family
just slapped you in the face

-how does it feel

somehow
I have
to go
and set
myself free
from this
roller coaster
of feelings
that you
have been giving me

there's this song
a certain song
that reminds me of you

made up memories
of ours that
I treasure so

songs don't get old
we do

sing for me
dance with me
make love to me

I tried
but I can't
forget you
won't stop thinking
about you
can't stop my heart
from loving you

it pains me
to see you
enjoying life
without me

it hurts me
to see you
happy with
someone else

I tried to
smile and hide
the pain
tried to throw it
far, far away
but it always
finds its way
back to me
but seeing you
with a smile on your face
gives me joy and assurance
that you are doing fine
even without me

I tried
you know
I did
I would have
ripped
my heart out
of my chest
if you wanted
me to

I had a choice
and I chose
to leave

I am a lot
stronger than you
wanted me to be

if you punched me
and expect me to
just stay there
and do nothing
you have misjudged me
for I will
punch you back
and maybe break
a finger or two
to teach you
that hurting someone
because they look weaker
than you
is a thing no
normal human would do

you ruined everything
I have worked for
and prayed for
ruined everything that I am

and it hit me like
lightning
you couldn't have done it
without me letting you do it

I was just too blind
to see that you were
trying to destroy me
not love me

I said forget him
but you won't listen

am I not the owner of my mind

I said stop loving him
but you won't listen

am I not the owner of my
heart

you did your best
but your best
didn't bring them happiness

I want you
need you
to explain
to me why
we ended up
like this

broken and full of hatred

I cried my heart out
when you left

you broke it to pieces
and never tried to fix it

I finally see what I am to you
your eyes – a window to
your soul
is telling me to go
for there's nothing left
between me and you

chapter 3

to find myself
I need to lose you

I am not alone
somewhere out there
there's someone like me
pouring their hearts out
to a typewriter

I was watching the moon
and tonight it smiled
and whispered to me
that the one that
I have been waiting for
is coming to carry me
to paradise
and wake my sleeping heart

she writes to forget the pain
not to forget you
but to forget the pain
you have caused her
and remember the love
you once have shared

if you think that they are
more
important than her

then let her live
the life she wanted to

just leave her
and be with them

don't tell her
what to think
don't tell her
what to do

her sprit's free
your thoughts
she doesn't need, no

I am nobody's woman

-I am my own woman

do you believe in good
goodbyes

I cry not because
I am weak
I cry because
I have loved

and someday
I will wipe these tears dry
and put a smile on my face

-I have loved and survived

I thought I'd never
cope with the pain
the day you left
and left me suffering

-I am happier now

giving up on you
is not an easy thing to do
you were everything
and nothing to me
a dream I have to let go

just love me
because you do
not because I hoped
and asked
that you feel
the same way too

you left me on a rainy day
he took me in the same day

he's been patient and kind
characteristics of a lover
that's hard to find

no, I am not coming back
I learned
to love the rain
when he came into my life

you and him are different
he's arrogant
and you were measured
he was loud
and you were quiet
but he was there to lift me
up
those times when I
needed you to care

knowing you
is one of the
biggest regrets
I've ever had

loving you
is the best - dumbest
thing I have ever done

and leaving you
is the best
decision I ever made
in my life

-thank you for the time
we have shared, I have
learned a lot

the sky cries
and the thunder
roars with me

you just don't belong to me
you are me

heart of mine, do what I say

this place has seen me
in the ugliest and prettiest
moments of my life
I don't want you changing it
you're an outsider
a nobody until I let you
in me but still
this is mine
and I do what I want
to do with it

-my body, my choice

his love can fade
but your love
for yourself won't

don't you see how gorgeous
the sunsets are
how pretty the rainbow is
after the rain
how beautiful a caterpillar
is when it turns to a
butterfly

just like you
today might not be yours
but tomorrow
you'll shine as bright as the
stars in the sky

don't tell me that dreams
never come true
you are here
with me and
and that itself is a dream
come true

let me take your hand
I'll hold it until forever

let me touch your face
I'll memorize every inch of it

let me kiss your lips
I'll seal our love with it

thank you for
coming into my life
at the right moment
and time
when I thought that love's
going to pass me by
for I have learned
not to trust
love and whoever offers it
you broke the wall
that I never realized
I built when I was hurting
the coldness in me
replaced with
warmth and understanding
you were there to show me
how big the world is
and how love moves in
mysterious ways

you have made bad decisions
did the same mistakes
you let them stomp you
and ruin your soul
which once was whole
and now you're standing up
cause all they can do is
try to break you
they didn't know
that every time they try to
you were there to try
and fix it up
they couldn't even see it
with their open eyes

your life is not insignificant
nobody's life is

don't let them decide
who you'll fall in love with

it's your life
your choice
your mistakes
your happiness
your dreams
your lover
your life

don't be scared of love
don't be afraid to love
love is glorious
in its ways and
yes when
there's love
there's pain
but the memories
stay with you
until the end

you are my home
in your arms
I feel safe
you have accepted me
and judged me
taught me
challenged me
believed in me
and ignored me
loved me and
hated me
but still you're
my home and
I miss you
oh so dearly

our scars
screams of our pains
and sufferings

their beauty stands out
to everyone who sees
for you are shining
and glowing like
never before

you are going to be judged
for every little thing you do
good or bad they are
going to hate you
they'd make you feel bad
to make themselves feel
better
do what you want
while you are still breathing
they don't matter
you do

-it's your life, not theirs

thank you note

Thank you! For giving a bit of your time
in reading this book.
Know that I really appreciate you.
Believe in yourself because you are
amazing.

-Frea Lee

about the book

Through words I am
showing
you a bit of my life.
What I have been through
and mostly
what I have seen.

about the author

I am a full-time housewife
and I am loving it
more than I imagined

Currently living in Texas
with my loving husband
and
our four-legged son

www.ingramcontent.com/pod-product-compliance
Lightning Source LLC
Chambersburg PA
CBHW061329040426
42444CB00011B/2833